W9-AGB-064

A SPECIAL GIFT

For:

....

From:

....

Date:

....

THE Greatest Moments

MAX LUCADO

COUNTRYMAN.

A Division of Word Publishing

Text copyright © 1995 by Max Lucado.
Illustrations copyright © 1995 by David Klein.
All rights reserved.
No portion of this book may be reproduced,
stored in a retrieval system, or transmitted in any
form or by any means—electronic, mechanical,
photocopy, recording, or any other—except for brief
quotations in printed reviews, without the prior
permission of the publisher.

All Scripture references are from the
New Century Version of the Bible,
copyright © 1987, 1988, 1991,
Word Publishing.
Used by permission.

Editorial development and design production
services by Koechel Peterson & Associates.

ISBN: 0-8499-5226-3

Printed in Hong Kong.

Contents

8 ~ Jesus' Birth Announced

10 ~ Jesus' Birth

12 ~ Jesus' Baptism and the Witness of John

16 ~ Jesus Begins His Ministry

18 ~ Jesus Calls Peter, James, and John

22 ~ Jesus Turns Water Into Wine at a Wedding

26 ~ Jesus Teaches Faith, Not Legalism

28 ~ Jesus' Sermon on the Mount

30 ~ Jesus Talks with a Samaritan Woman

34 ~ Jesus Heals a Paralyzed Man

37 ~ Jesus Raises a Widow's Son

38 ~ Jesus Heals Jairus' Daughter

40 ~ Jesus Heals a Sick Woman

42 ~ Jesus Affirms John the Baptist

44 ~ Jesus Casts Out a Mute Spirit

48 ~ Jesus' Transfiguration

50 ~ Jesus Heals a Man at the Pool of Bethesda

52 ~ Jesus Feeds Five Thousand People

54 ~ Jesus Walks on Water

58 ~ Jesus Forgives the Woman Taken in Adultery

60 ~ Jesus Heals a Canaanite Woman's Daughter

62 ~ Jesus Teaches Forgiveness

Contents

65 ~ Jesus Heals Ten Lepers

68 ~ Jesus Answers a Rich Man

70 ~ Jesus Heals a Blind Man

72 ~ Jesus Raises Lazarus
from the Dead

74 ~ Mary Washes Jesus'
Feet with Her Hair

77 ~ The Triumphal Entry

80 ~ The Lesson of the Fig Tree

83 ~ Jesus Clears the Temple

85 ~ Jesus Washes His
Disciples' Feet

88 ~ The Last Supper

90 ~ Jesus Reveals His Authority

94 ~ Jesus Proclaims His Victory
Over the World

96 ~ Jesus Prays in the
Garden of Gethsemane

99 ~ Jesus Is Arrested

101 ~ Pilate Questions Jesus

105 ~ The Repentant Thief

108 ~ Jesus' Crucifixion

111 ~ The Resurrection

113 ~ The Road to Emmaus

116 ~ Jesus Calls Paul

119 ~ A View of Heaven

123 ~ Your Greatest Moment

126 ~ Acknowledgments

Introduction

Simple moments. Quiet moments.

*Moments missed by many, but created by God,
forever punctuating the timeline of history.*

You can't open the Gospels without reading about them.

They are the greatest moments:

~ *Mary watches her baby boy in a feed trough and ponders,
"How can this really be God?"*

~ *The apostles stare at a lunchbucket of loaves
and fish that never goes empty.*

~ *A leper sees new fingers appear where only nubs had been
and runs back to thank his God.*

~ *God does what he would be doing only in your wildest dreams—
wearing diapers, riding donkeys, washing feet, dozing in storms,
and dying for your sins.*

*These are The Greatest Moments, when God put on humanity,
not only to save us from our sins but to experience life as we do,
with all its laughter and tears.*

JESUS' BIRTH ANNOUNCED

*During Elizabeth's sixth month of pregnancy, God sent the angel
Gabriel to Nazareth, a town in Galilee, to a virgin. She was engaged to marry a man
named Joseph from the family of David. Her name was Mary. The angel came to
her and said, "Greetings! The Lord has blessed you and is with you."*

But Mary was very startled by what the angel said and wondered what this greeting might mean.

*The angel said to her, "Don't be afraid, Mary; God has shown you his grace. Listen! You will
become pregnant and give birth to a son, and you will name him Jesus. He will be great and
will be called the Son of the Most High. The Lord God will give him the throne of King David,
his ancestor. He will rule over the people of Jacob forever, and his kingdom will never end."*

Mary said to the angel, "How will this happen since I am a virgin?"

*The angel said to Mary, "The Holy Spirit will come upon you, and the power of the Most High
will cover you. For this reason the baby will be holy and will be called the Son of God."*

LUKE 1:26-35

MAX LUCADO

One

*G*abriel was never one to question, but this time he had to wonder.

God will become a baby? Gabriel had seen babies before. He had been platoon leader on the bulrush operation. He remembered what little Moses looked like.

That's okay for humans, he thought to himself. *But God?* The heavens can't contain him; how could a body?

And what of this name—what was it—*Jesus?* Such a common name. Come on, even *Gabriel* has more punch to it than *Jesus.*

So Gabriel scratched his head. What happened to the good ol' days? The Sodom and Gomorrah stuff. Flooding the globe. Flaming swords. That's the action he liked.

But Gabriel had his orders. Take the message to Mary. *Must be a special girl,* he assumed as he traveled. But Gabriel was in for another shock. The mother-to-be of God was not regal. She was a Jewish peasant who'd barely outgrown her acne and had a crush on a guy named Joe.

And speaking of Joe—what does this fellow know? You're telling me the source of wisdom is going to call this guy "Dad"?

It was all Gabriel could do to keep from turning back. "This is a peculiar idea you have, God," he must have muttered to himself.

Are God's guardians given to such musings? Are we? Only heaven knows how long Gabriel fluttered unseen above Mary before he took a breath and broke the news. But he did. He told her the name. He told her the plan. He told her not to be afraid. And when he announced, "With God nothing is impossible!" he said it as much for himself as for her.

For even though he couldn't answer the questions, he knew who could, and that was enough.

JESUS' BIRTH

The Word became a human and lived among us. We saw his glory—
that belongs to the only Son of the Father—and he was full of grace and truth.…

Because he was full of grace and truth, from him we all received one gift after another.
The law was given through Moses, but grace and truth came through Jesus Christ.
No one has ever seen God. But God the only Son is very close to the Father,
and he has shown us what God is like.

JOHN 1:14-18

*I*t all happened in a moment, a most remarkable moment that was like none other. For through that segment of time a spectacular thing occurred. God became a man. While the creatures of earth walked unaware, Divinity arrived. Heaven opened herself and placed her most precious one in a human womb.

God as a fetus. Holiness sleeping in a womb. The creator of life being created.

God was given eyebrows, elbows, two kidneys, and a spleen. He stretched against the walls and floated in the amniotic fluids of his mother.

God had come near. No silk. No ivory. No hype. To think of Jesus in such a light is—well, it seems almost irreverent, doesn't it. It is much easier to keep the humanity out of the incarnation.

But don't do it. For heaven's sake, don't. Let him be as human as he intended to be. Let him into the mire and muck of our world. For only if we let him in can he pull us out.

MAX LUCADO
FROM: *GOD CAME NEAR*

JESUS' BIRTH

JESUS' BAPTISM AND
THE WITNESS OF JOHN

Some Pharisees who had been sent asked John:
"If you are not the Christ or Elijah or the Prophet, why do you baptize people?"

John answered, "I baptize with water, but there is one here with you
that you don't know about. He is the One who comes after me. I am not
good enough to untie the strings of his sandals."

This all happened at Bethany on the other side of the Jordan River,
where John was baptizing people.

MAX LUCADO

The next day John saw Jesus coming toward him. John said,
"Look, the Lamb of God, who takes away the sin of the world! This is the
One I was talking about when I said, 'A man will come after me, but he is greater than
I am, because he was living before me.' Even I did not know who he was, although
I came baptizing with water so that the people of Israel would know who he is."

Then John said, "I saw the Spirit come down from heaven in the form of
a dove and rest on him. Until then I did not know who the Christ was. But the God
who sent me to baptize with water told me, 'You will see the Spirit come down and rest
on a man; he is the One who will baptize with the Holy Spirit.' I have seen this happen,
and I tell you the truth: This man is the Son of God."

JOHN 1:24-34

John the Baptist saw a dove and believed. James Whittaker saw a sea gull and believed. James Whittaker was a member of the hand-picked crew that flew the B-17 Flying Fortress captained by Eddie Rickenbacker. Anybody who remembers October of 1942 remembers the day Rickenbacker and his crew were reported lost at sea.

Somewhere over the Pacific, out of radio range, the plane ran out of fuel and crashed into the ocean. The nine men spent the next months floating in three rafts. They battled the heat, the storms, and the water. Sharks, some ten feet long, would ram their nine-foot boats. After only eight days their rations were eaten or destroyed by saltwater. It would take a miracle to survive.

One morning after their daily devotions, Rickenbacker leaned his head back against the raft and pulled his hat over his eyes. A bird landed on his head. He peered out from under his hat. Every eye was on him. He instinctively knew it was a sea gull.

Rickenbacker caught it, and the crew ate it. The bird's intestines were used for bait to catch fish…and the crew survived to tell the story. A story about a stranded crew with no hope or help in sight. A story about prayers offered and prayers answered. A story of salvation.

You may have heard the Rickenbacker

Three

story before. You may have read it in one of my books. Coreen Schweenk did. After reading this story in my book *In the Eye of the Storm,* Mrs. Schweenk felt compelled to write to me. The real miracle, she informed me, was not a bird on the head of Eddie Rickenbacker but a change in the heart of James Whittaker. The greatest event of that day was not the rescue of a crew but the rescue of a soul.

James Whittaker was an unbeliever. The plane crash didn't change his unbelief. The days facing death didn't cause him to reconsider his destiny. In fact, Mrs. Whittaker said her husband grew irritated with John Bartak, a crew member who continually read his Bible privately and aloud.

But his protests didn't stop Bartak from reading. Nor did Whittaker's resistance stop the Word from penetrating his soul. Unknown to Whittaker, the soil of his heart was being plowed. For it was one morning after a Bible reading that the sea gull landed on Captain Rickenbacker's head. And at that moment Jim became a believer.

I chuckled when I read the letter. Not at the letter; I believe every word of it. Nor at James Whittaker. But I had to chuckle at...please excuse me...I had to chuckle at God. Isn't that just like him? Who would go to such extremes to save a soul? Amazing the lengths to which God will go to get our attention.

JESUS BEGINS HIS MINISTRY

*When Jesus heard that John had been put in prison,
he went back to Galilee. He left Nazareth and went to live in Capernaum,
a town near Lake Galilee, in the area near Zebulun and Naphtali. Jesus did this
to bring about what the prophet Isaiah had said: "Land of Zebulun and land of
Naphtali along the sea, beyond the Jordan River. This is Galilee where the non-Jewish
people live. These people who live in darkness will see a great light. They live in
a place covered with the shadows of death, but a light will shine on them."*

MATTHEW 4:12-16

Four

He looked around the carpentry shop. He stood for a moment in the refuge of the little room that housed so many sweet memories. He balanced the hammer in his hand. He ran his fingers across the sharp teeth of the saw. He stroked the smoothly worn wood of the sawhorse. He had come to say good-bye.

It was time for him to leave. He had heard something that made him know it was time to go. So he came one last time to smell the sawdust and lumber. Life was peaceful here. Life was so…safe.

I wonder what he thought as he took one last look around the room. Perhaps he stood for a moment. Perhaps he listened as voices from the past filled the air. "Good job, Jesus." "Joseph, Jesus—come and eat!" "Don't worry, sir, we'll get it finished on time. I'll get Jesus to help me." I wonder if he hesitated.

You can almost see the tools of the trade in his words as he spoke. You can see the trueness of a plumb line as he called for moral standards. You can imagine him with a pencil and a ledger as he urges honesty. It was here that his human hands shaped the wood his divine hands had created. And it was here that his body matured while his spirit waited for the right moment, the right day.

And now that day had arrived.

JESUS CALLS PETER, JAMES, AND JOHN

When Jesus had finished speaking, he said to Simon, "Take the boat into deep water, and put your nets in the water to catch some fish."

Simon answered, "Master, we worked hard all night trying to catch fish, and we caught nothing. But you say to put the nets in the water, so I will." When the fishermen did as Jesus told them, they caught so many fish that the nets began to break. They called to their partners in the other boat to come and help them. They came and filled both boats so full that they were almost sinking.

When Simon Peter saw what had happened, he bowed down before Jesus and said, "Go away from me, Lord. I am a sinful man!" He and the other fishermen were amazed at the many fish they caught, as were James and John, the sons of Zebedee, Simon's partners.

Jesus said to Simon, "Don't be afraid. From now on you will fish for people." When the men brought their boats to the shore, they left everything and followed Jesus.

LUKE 5:4-11

Five

*P*ush out into the deep, Peter. Let's fish."

I groaned. I looked at John. We were thinking the same thing. As long as he wanted to use the boat for a platform to speak, that was fine. But to use it for a fishing boat—that was our territory. I started to tell this carpenter-teacher, "You stick to preaching, and I'll stick to fishing." But I was more polite: "We worked all night. We didn't catch a thing."

I wish I could say I did it because of love. I wish I could say I did it out of devotion. But I can't. All I can say is there is a time to question and a time to listen.

With every pull of the paddle, I grumbled. "No way. No way. Impossible. I may not know much, but I know fishing. And all we're going to come back with are some wet nets."

Finally we cast anchor. I picked up the heavy netting, held it waist-high, and started to throw it. That's when I caught a glimpse of Jesus out of the corner of my eye. His expression stopped me in mid-motion.

He noticed me looking at him, and he tried to hide the smile, but it persisted. It pushed at the corners of his mouth until a flash of teeth appeared. He had given me a gift and could scarcely contain himself as I opened it.

"Boy, is he in for a disappointment," I thought as I threw the net. I wrapped the rope once around my hand and sat back for the long wait.

But there was no wait. The slack rope yanked taut and tried to pull me overboard. I set my feet against the side of the boat and yelled for help.

We got the net in just before it began to tear. I'd never seen such a catch. We began to take in water. John screamed for the other boat to help us.

It was quite a scene: four fishermen in two boats, knee-deep in fish, and one carpenter seated on our bow, relishing the pandemonium.

That's when I realized who he was. And that's when I realized who I was: I was the one who told God what he couldn't do!

"Go away from me, Lord; I'm a sinful man." There wasn't anything else I could say.

I don't know what he saw in me, but he didn't leave. Maybe he thought if I would let him tell me how to fish, I would let him tell me how to live.

It was a scene I would see many times over the next couple of years—in cemeteries with the dead, on hillsides with the hungry, in storms with the frightened, on roadsides with the sick. The characters would change, but the theme wouldn't. When we would say, "No way," he would say, "My way." Then the ones who doubted would scramble to salvage the blessing. And the One who gave it would savor the surprise.

MAX LUCADO
FROM: *THE APPLAUSE OF HEAVEN*

JESUS CALLS PETER, JAMES AND JOHN

JESUS TURNS WATER INTO WINE AT A WEDDING

Two days later there was a wedding in the town of Cana in Galilee. Jesus' mother was there, and Jesus and his followers were also invited to the wedding. When all the wine was gone, Jesus' mother said to him, "They have no more wine."

Jesus answered, "Dear woman, why come to me? My time has not yet come."

His mother said to the servants, "Do whatever he tells you to do."

In that place there were six stone water jars that the Jews used in their washing ceremony. Each jar held about twenty or thirty gallons.

Jesus said to the servants, "Fill the jars with water." So they filled the jars to the top.

Then he said to them, "Now take some out and give it to the master of the feast."

So they took the water to the master. When he tasted it, the water had become wine. He did not know where the wine came from, but the servants who had brought the water knew. The master of the wedding called the bridegroom and said to him, "People always serve the best wine first. Later, after the guests have been drinking awhile, they serve the cheaper wine. But you have saved the best wine till now."

So in Cana of Galilee Jesus did his first miracle. There he showed his glory, and his followers believed in him.

John 2:1-11

wedding in the time of Christ was no small event. It usually began with a sundown ceremony at the synagogue. People would then leave the synagogue and begin a long, candlelight procession through the city, winding their way through the soft evening sunlight of the city streets. The couple would be escorted past as many homes as possible so everyone could wish them well. After the processional, however, the couple didn't go on a honeymoon; the honeymoon was brought to them.

They would go home to a party. For several days there would be gift-giving, speechmaking, food-eating and—you guessed it!—wine-drinking. Food and wine were taken very seriously. The host honored the guests by keeping their plates full and their cups overflowing. It was considered an insult to the guests if the host ran out of food or wine.

Hospitality at a wedding was a sacred duty. So serious were these social customs that, if they were not observed, lawsuits could be brought by the injured parties!

"Without wine," said the rabbis, "there is no joy." Wine was crucial, not for drunkenness, which was considered a disgrace, but for what it demonstrated. The presence of wine stated that this was a special day and that all the guests were special guests.

The absence of wine, then, was a social embarrassment.

Mary, the mother of Jesus, is one of the first to notice that the wine has run out.

MAX LUCADO

She goes to her son and points out the problem: "They have no more wine."

Jesus' response? "Dear woman, why come to me? My time has not yet come."

Interesting statement. "My time." Jesus is aware of the plan. He has a place and a time for his first miracle. And this isn't it.

Jesus knows the plan. At first, it appears he is going to stay with it. But as he hears his mother and looks into the faces of the wedding party, he reconsiders. The significance of the plan is slowly eclipsed by his concern for the people. Timing is important, but people are more so.

As a result, he changes his plan to meet the needs of some friends. Incredible. The schedule of heaven is altered so some friends won't be embarrassed. The inaugural miracle is motivated—not by tragedy or famine or moral collapse—but by concern for friends who are in a bind.

Why did Jesus do it? What motivated his first miracle?

His friends were embarrassed. What bothered them bothered him.

So go ahead. Tell God what hurts. Talk to him. He won't turn you away. He won't think it's silly. "For our high priest is *able to understand* our weaknesses. When he lived on earth, he was tempted in every way that we are, but he did not sin. Let us, then, feel very sure that we can come before God's throne where there is grace" (Heb. 4:15-16, emphasis added).

Does God care about the little things in our lives? You better believe it.

If it matters to you, it matters to him.

JESUS TEACHES FAITH, NOT LEGALISM

There was a man named Nicodemus who was one of the Pharisees and an important Jewish leader. One night Nicodemus came to Jesus and said, "Teacher, we know you are a teacher sent from God, because no one can do the miracles you do unless God is with him."

Jesus answered, "I tell you the truth, unless one is born again, he cannot be in God's kingdom."

Nicodemus said, "But if a person is already old, how can he be born again? He cannot enter his mother's body again. So how can a person be born a second time?"

But Jesus answered, "I tell you the truth, unless one is born from water and the Spirit, he cannot enter God's kingdom. Human life comes from human parents, but spiritual life comes from the Spirit."

JOHN 3:1-6

MAX LUCADO

Nicodemus is drawn to the carpenter, but he can't be seen with him. Nicodemus is on the high court. He can't approach Jesus in the day. So Nicodemus goes to meet him at night. He goes in the darkness. Appropriate. For legalism offers no light.

That's legalism. It's rigid. It's mechanical—and it's not from God.

Can I give you the down and dirty about legalism? Legalism doesn't need God. Legalism is the search for innocence—not forgiveness. It's a systematic process of defending self, explaining self, exalting self, and justifying self. Legalists are obsessed with self—not God.

Legalism:

~Turns my opinion into your burden.

There is only room for one opinion in the boat. And guess who is wrong!

~Turns my opinion into your boundary. Your opposing opinion makes me question not only your right to have fellowship with me, but also your salvation.

~Turns my opinion into your obligation. Christians must toe the company line. Your job isn't to think, it's to march.

If you want to be in the group, stay in step and don't ask questions.

Nicodemus knew how to march, but he longed to sing. He knew there was something more, but he didn't know where to find it. So he went to Jesus.

JESUS' SERMON ON THE MOUNT

When Jesus saw the crowds, he went up on a hill and sat down. His followers came to him, and he began to teach them, saying:

"Those people who know they have great spiritual needs are happy, because the kingdom of heaven belongs to them.

Those who are sad now are happy, because God will comfort them.

Those who are humble are happy, because the earth will belong to them.

Those who want to do right more than anything else are happy, because God will fully satisfy them.

Those who show mercy to others are happy, because God will show mercy to them.

Those who are pure in their thinking are happy, because they will be with God.

Those who work to bring peace are happy, because God will call them his children.

Those who are treated badly for doing good are happy, because the kingdom of heaven belongs to them."

MATTHEW 5:1-10

MAX LUCADO

Eight

*S*acred delight is good news coming through the back door of your heart. It's what you'd always dreamed but never expected. It's having God as your pinch-hitter, your lawyer, your dad, your biggest fan, and your best friend. It's hope where you least expected it: a flower in life's sidewalk.

And it is this sacred delight that Jesus promises in the Sermon on the Mount.

Nine times he promises it. And he promises it to an unlikely crowd:

~ *"The poor in spirit."* Beggars in God's soup kitchen.

~ *"Those who mourn."* Sinners Anonymous bound together by the truth of their introduction: "Hi, I am me. I'm a sinner."

~ *"The meek."* Pawnshop pianos played by Van Cliburn. (He's so good no one notices the missing keys.)

~ *"Those who hunger and thirst."* Famished orphans who know the difference between a TV dinner and a Thanksgiving feast.

~ *"The merciful."* Winners of the million-dollar lottery who share the prize with their enemies.

~ *"The pure in heart."* Physicians who love lepers and escape infection.

~ *"The peacemakers."* Architects who build bridges with wood from a Roman cross.

~ *"The persecuted."* Those who manage to keep an eye on heaven while walking through hell on earth.

It is to this band of pilgrims that God promises a special blessing. A heavenly joy. A sacred delight.

JESUS TALKS WITH
A SAMARITAN WOMAN

In Samaria Jesus came to the town called Sychar, which is near the field Jacob gave to his son Joseph. Jacob's well was there. Jesus was tired from his long trip, so he sat down beside the well. It was about twelve o'clock noon. When a Samaritan woman came to the well to get some water, Jesus said to her, "Please give me a drink." (This happened while Jesus' followers were in town buying some food.)

The woman said, "I am surprised that you ask me for a drink, since you are a Jewish man and I am a Samaritan woman." (Jewish people are not friends with Samaritans.)

Jesus said, "If you only knew the free gift of God and who it is that is asking you for water, you would have asked him, and he would have given you living water."

The woman said, "Sir, where will you get this living water? The well is very deep, and you have nothing to get water with. Are you greater than Jacob, our father, who gave us this well and drank from it himself along with his sons and flocks?"

Jesus answered, "Everyone who drinks this water will be thirsty again, but whoever drinks the water I give will never be thirsty. The water I give will become a spring of water gushing up inside that person, giving eternal life."

The woman said to him, "Sir, give me this water so I will never be thirsty again and will not have to come back here to get more water."

Jesus told her, "Go get your husband and come back here."

The woman answered, "I have no husband."

Jesus said to her, "You are right to say you have no husband. Really you have had five husbands, and the man you live with now is not your husband. You told the truth."

The woman said, "Sir, I can see that you are a prophet. Our ancestors worshiped on this mountain, but you Jews say that Jerusalem is the place where people must worship."

Jesus said, "Believe me, woman. The time is coming when neither in Jerusalem nor on this mountain will you actually worship the Father. You Samaritans worship something you don't understand. We understand what we worship, because salvation comes from the Jews. The time is coming when the true worshipers will worship the Father in spirit and truth, and that time is here already. You see, the Father too is actively seeking such people to worship him. God is spirit, and those who worship him must worship in spirit and truth."

The woman said, "I know that the Messiah is coming." (Messiah is the One called Christ.) "When the Messiah comes, he will explain everything to us."

Then Jesus said, "I am he—I, the one talking to you."

JOHN 4:5-26

*H*e was seated on the ground: legs outstretched, hands folded, back resting against the well. She stopped and looked at him. He was obviously Jewish. What was he doing here?

Sensing her discomfort, Jesus asked her for water. But she was too streetwise to think that all he wanted was a drink. She wanted to know what he really had in mind. Her intuition was partly correct. He was interested in her heart.

They talked. Who could remember the last time a man had spoken to her with respect? He told her about a spring of water that would quench, not the thirst of the throat, but of the soul.

"Sir, give me this water so that I won't get thirsty and have to keep coming here to draw water."

"Go, call your husband and come back."

Her heart must have sunk. Here was a Jew who didn't care if she was a Samaritan. Here was the closest thing to gentleness she'd ever seen. And now he was asking her about…that. Anything but that.

"I have no husband." (Kindness has a way of inviting honesty.) This woman wondered what Jesus would do. He will be angry. He will leave. He will think I'm worthless. If you've had the same anxieties, then get out your pencil. You'll want to underline Jesus' answer. "You're right. You have had five husbands and the man you are with now won't even give you a name."

No criticism? No anger? No what-kind-of-mess-have-your-made-of-your-life lectures? The woman was amazed. "I can see you are a prophet."

Then she asked the question that revealed the gaping hole in her soul. "Where is God? My people say he is on the mountain. Your people say he is in Jerusalem. I don't know where he is." I'd give a thousand sunsets to see the expression on Jesus' face as he heard those words. Of all the women to have an insatiable appetite for God—a five-time divorcée? And of all the people to be chosen to personally receive the secret of the ages— an outcast among outcasts? Remarkable. His eyes must have danced as he whispered the secret. "I am the Messiah."

"Then, leaving her water jar, the woman went back to the town and said to the people, 'Come, see a man who told me everything I ever did. Could this be the Christ?'" Did you notice what she forgot? She forgot her water jar. She left behind the jug that had caused the sag in her shoulders. She left behind the burden she brought. Suddenly the shame of the tattered romances disappeared. Suddenly the insignificance of her life was swallowed by the significance of the moment. "God is here! God has come! God cares for me!"

JESUS HEALS A PARALYZED MAN

A few days later, when Jesus came back to Capernaum, the news spread that he was at home. Many people gathered together so that there was no room in the house, not even outside the door. And Jesus was teaching them God's message. Four people came, carrying a paralyzed man. Since they could not get to Jesus because of the crowd, they dug a hole in the roof right above where he was speaking. When they got through, they lowered the mat with the paralyzed man on it. When Jesus saw the faith of these people, he said to the paralyzed man, "Young man, your sins are forgiven."

Immediately the paralyzed man stood up, took his mat, and walked out while everyone was watching him.

The people were amazed and praised God. They said, "We have never seen anything like this!"

MARK 2:1-5, 12

MAX LUCADO

It was risky—they could fall. It was dangerous—*he* could fall. It was unorthodox—de-roofing is antisocial. It was intrusive—Jesus was busy. But it was their only chance to see Jesus. So they climbed to the roof.

Faith does those things. Faith does the unexpected. And faith gets God's attention. Look what Mark says: "When Jesus saw the faith of these people, he said to the paralyzed man, 'Young man, your sins are forgiven.'"

The friends want him to heal their friend. But Jesus won't settle for a simple healing of the body—he wants to heal the soul. He leapfrogs the physical and deals with the spiritual. To heal the body is temporal; to heal the soul is eternal.

The request of the friends is valid—but timid. The expectations of the crowd are high—but not high enough. They expect Jesus to say, "I heal you." Instead he says, "I forgive you."

They expect him to treat the body, for that is what they see.

He chooses to treat not only the body, but also the spiritual, for that is what he sees.

They want Jesus to give the man a new body so he can walk. Jesus gives grace so the man can live.

Remarkable. Sometimes God is so touched by what he sees that he gives us what we need and not simply that for which we ask.

JESUS RAISES A WIDOW'S SON

Eleven

JESUS RAISES A WIDOW'S SON

Soon afterwards Jesus went to a town called Nain, and his followers and a large crowd traveled with him. When he came near the town gate, he saw a funeral. A mother, who was a widow, had lost her only son. A large crowd from the town was with the mother while her son was being carried out. When the Lord saw her, he felt very sorry for her and said, "Don't cry." He went up and touched the coffin, and the people who were carrying it stopped. Jesus said, "Young man, I tell you, get up!" And the son sat up and began to talk. Then Jesus gave him back to his mother.

All the people were amazed and began praising God, saying, "A great prophet has come to us! God has come to help his people."

LUKE 7:11-16

The mourners didn't cause him to stop. Nor did the large crowd, or even the body of the dead man on the stretcher. It was the woman—the look on her face and the redness in her eyes. He knew immediately what was happening. It was her son who was being carried out, her only son. And if anyone knows the pain that comes from losing your only son, God does.

So he did it; he went into action. "Don't cry," he told the mother. "Arise!" he told the boy. The dead man spoke, the devil ran, and the people were reminded of this truth: For those who know the Author of Life, death is nothing more than Satan's dead-man's bluff.

JESUS HEALS JAIRUS' DAUGHTER

A leader of the synagogue, named Jairus . . . begged Jesus, saying again and again, "My daughter is dying. Please come and put your hands on her so she will be healed and will live." So Jesus went with him.

When they came to the house of the synagogue leader, Jesus found many people there making lots of noise and crying loudly. Jesus entered the house and said to them, "Why are you crying and making so much noise? The child is not dead, only asleep.". . . Taking hold of the girl's hand, he said to her, "Talitha, koum!" (This means, "Young girl, I tell you to stand up!")
At once the girl stood right up and began walking. (She was twelve years old.)
Everyone was completely amazed.

MARK 5:22-24, 38-42

MAX LUCADO

*J*airus is the leader of the synagogue. That may not mean much to you and me, but in the days of Christ the leader of the synagogue was the most important man in the community. The synagogue was the center of religion, education, leadership, and social activity. The leader of the synagogue was the senior religious leader, the highest-ranking professor, the mayor, and the best-known citizen all in one.

Who could ask for more? Yet Jairus does. He has to ask for more. In fact, he would trade the whole package of perks and privileges for just one assurance—that his daughter will live.

He fell at Jesus' feet, "saying again and again, 'My daughter is dying. Please come and put your hands on her so she will be healed and will live.' "

He doesn't barter with Jesus. He doesn't negotiate with Jesus. He doesn't make excuses. He just pleads.

There are times in life when everything you have to offer is nothing compared to what you are asking to receive. What could a man offer in exchange for his child's life? So there are no games. No haggling. No masquerades.

So Jairus asks for his help. And Jesus, who loves the honest heart, goes to give it.

JESUS HEALS A SICK WOMAN

A large crowd followed Jesus and pushed very close around him. Among them was a woman who had been bleeding for twelve years. She had suffered very much from many doctors and had spent all the money she had, but instead of improving, she was getting worse. When the woman heard about Jesus, she came up behind him in the crowd and touched his coat. She thought, "If I can just touch his clothes, I will be healed." Instantly her bleeding stopped, and she felt in her body that she was healed from her disease.

At once Jesus felt power go out from him. So he turned around in the crowd and asked, "Who touched my clothes?"

His followers said, "Look at how many people are pushing against you! And you ask, 'Who touched me?'"

But Jesus continued looking around to see who had touched him. The woman, knowing that she was healed, came and fell at Jesus' feet. Shaking with fear, she told him the whole truth. Jesus said to her, "Dear woman, you are made well because you believed. Go in peace; be healed of your disease."

MARK 5:24-34

MAX LUCADO

She was a bruised reed: "bleeding for twelve years," "suffered very much," "spent all the money she had," and "getting worse." But for a Jewess, nothing could be worse. No part of her life was left unaffected.

Sexually...she could not touch her husband.

Maternally...she could not bear children.

Domestically...anything she touched was considered unclean. No washing dishes, sweeping floors.

Spiritually...she was not allowed to enter the temple.

She was physically exhausted and socially ostracized.

By the time she gets to Jesus, he is surrounded by people. "If I can just touch his clothes," she thinks, "I will be healed." Risky decision. To touch him, she will have to touch the people. If one of them recognizes her, hello rebuke, good-bye cure. But what choice does she have? All she has is a crazy hunch that Jesus can help and a high hope that he will.

Maybe that's all you have: a crazy hunch and a high hope. You have nothing to give. Maybe that has kept you from coming to God. If that describes you, note carefully, only one person was commended that day for having faith. She was a shame-struck, penniless outcast who clutched onto her hunch that he could and her hope that he would.

JESUS AFFIRMS
JOHN THE BAPTIST

As John's followers were leaving, Jesus began talking to the people about John. Jesus said, "What did you go out into the desert to see? A reed blown by the wind? What did you go out to see? A man dressed in fine clothes? No, those who wear fine clothes live in kings' palaces. So why did you go out? To see a prophet? Yes, and I tell you, John is more than a prophet. This was written about him: 'I will send my messenger ahead of you, who will prepare the way for you.'

I tell you the truth, John the Baptist is greater than any other person ever born, but even the least important person in the kingdom of heaven is greater than John."

MATTHEW 11:7-11

John the Baptist would never get hired today. He was a public relations disaster. He "wore clothes made from camels' hair, had a leather belt around his waist, and ate locusts and wild honey" (Mark 1:6). Who would want to look at a guy like that every Sunday?

His message was as rough as his dress: a no-nonsense, bare-fisted challenge to repent because God was on his way. Didn't matter to John if you were a Jew, a priest, a Baptist, or all three. No, John would never get hired today. His tactics lacked tact. His style wasn't smooth. He made few friends and lots of enemies, but what do you know? He made hundreds of converts. "All the people from Judea and Jerusalem were going out to him. They confessed their sins and were baptized by him in the Jordan River" (Mark 1:5).

Look at that. "All the people of Judea and Jerusalem...". How do we explain such a response? It certainly wasn't his charisma or clothing. Nor was it his money or position, for he had neither. Then what did he have? One word. *Holiness.* He reminded his hearers of Elijah. And he reminds us of this truth: "There is winsomeness in holiness." You don't have to be like the world to have an impact on the world. You don't have to be like the crowd to change the crowd. You don't have to lower yourself down to their level to lift them up to your level.

You want to make a difference in your world? Live a holy life: Don't speak one message and live another.

JESUS CASTS OUT A MUTE SPIRIT

When Jesus, Peter, James, and John came back to the other followers, they saw a great crowd around them and the teachers of the law arguing with them. But as soon as the crowd saw Jesus, the people were surprised and ran to welcome him.

Jesus asked, "What are you arguing about?"

A man answered, "Teacher, I brought my son to you. He has an evil spirit in him that stops him from talking…. I asked your followers to force the evil spirit out, but they couldn't."

…So the followers brought him to Jesus. As soon as the evil spirit saw Jesus, it made the boy lose control of himself, and he fell down and rolled on the ground, foaming at the mouth.

Jesus asked the boy's father, "How long has this been happening?" The father answered, "Since he was very young. The spirit often throws him into a fire or into water to kill him. If you can do anything for him, please have pity on us and help us."

*Jesus said to the father, "You said, 'If you can!' All things are possible
for the one who believes."*

Immediately the father cried out, "I do believe! Help me to believe more!"

*When Jesus saw that a crowd was quickly gathering, he ordered the evil
spirit, saying, "You spirit that makes people unable to hear or speak, I command
you to come out of this boy and never enter him again!" The evil spirit screamed and
caused the boy to fall on the ground again. Then the spirit came out. The boy
looked as if he were dead, and many people said, "He is dead!" But Jesus took
hold of the boy's hand and helped him to stand up.*

*When Jesus went into the house, his followers began asking him privately,
"Why couldn't we force that evil spirit out?" Jesus answered, "That kind
of spirit can only be forced out by prayer."*

MARK 9:14-29

*I*f you struggle with prayer, I've got just the guy for you. Don't worry, he's not a monastic saint. He's not a calloused-kneed apostle. Nor is he a prophet whose middle name is Meditation. He's not a too-holy-to-be-you reminder of how far you need to go in prayer. He's just the opposite. A parent with a sick son in need of a miracle. The father's prayer isn't much, but the answer is and the result reminds us: The power is not in the prayer; it's in the one who hears it.

He prayed out of desperation. His son, his only son, was demon-possessed. Not only was he a deaf mute and an epileptic, he was also possessed by an evil spirit. Ever since the boy was young, the demon had thrown him into fires and water.

Imagine the pain of the father. Other dads could watch their children grow and mature; he could only watch his suffer. While others were teaching their sons an occupation, he was just trying to keep his son alive.

What a challenge! He couldn't leave his son alone for a minute. Who knew when the next attack would come? The father had to remain on call, on alert twenty-four hours a day. He was desperate and tired, and his prayer reflects both.

"If you can do anything for him, please have pity on us and help us."

Listen to that prayer. Does it sound courageous? Confident? Strong? Hardly.

One word would have made a lot of difference. Instead of *if*, what if he'd said *since*? "Since you can do anything for him, please have pity on us and help us."

MAX LUCADO

But that's not what he said. He said *if*. The Greek is even more emphatic. The tense implies doubt. It's as if the man were saying, "This one's probably out of your league, but if you can…"

More meek than mighty. More timid than towering. More like a crippled lamb coming to a shepherd than a proud lion roaring in the jungle. If his prayer sounds like yours, then don't be discouraged, for that's where prayer begins.

It begins as a yearning. An honest appeal. Ordinary people staring at Mount Everest. No pretense. No boasting. No posturing. Just prayer. Feeble prayer, but prayer nonetheless.

We are tempted to wait to pray until we know how to pray. We've heard the prayers of the spiritually mature. We've read of the rigors of the disciplined. And we are convinced we've a long way to traverse.

And since we'd rather not pray than pray poorly, we don't pray. Or we pray infrequently. We are waiting to pray until we learn how to pray.

Good thing this man didn't make the same mistake. He wasn't much of a prayer. And his wasn't much of a prayer. He even admits it! "I do believe," he implored. "Help me to believe more" (see Mark 9:24).

This prayer isn't destined for a worship manual. But Jesus responded. He responded, not to the eloquence of the man, but to the pain of the man.

JESUS' TRANSFIGURATION

About eight days after Jesus said these things, he took Peter, John, and James and went up on a mountain to pray. While Jesus was praying, the appearance of his face changed, and his clothes became shining white. Then two men, Moses and Elijah, were talking with Jesus. They appeared in heavenly glory, talking about his departure which he would soon bring about in Jerusalem. Peter and the others were very sleepy, but when they awoke fully, they saw the glory of Jesus and the two men standing with him. When Moses and Elijah were about to leave, Peter said to Jesus, "Master it is good that we are here. Let us make three tents—one for you, one for Moses, and one for Elijah." (Peter did not know what he was talking about.)

While he was saying these things, a cloud came and covered them, and they became afraid as the cloud covered them. A voice came from the cloud, saying, "This is my Son, whom I have chosen. Listen to him!"

When the voice finished speaking, only Jesus was there. Peter, John, and James said nothing and told no one at that time what they had seen.

LUKE 9:28-36

MAX LUCADO

"As he was praying," Luke writes, "the appearance of his face changed, and his clothes became as bright as a flash of lightning." For just a moment, he is transfigured; a roaring radiance pours from him. He becomes as he was before he came. He is elevated above earth's horizon and escorted into the eternal. He is home again. Familiar sounds surround him.

Moses and Elijah, aflame with eternal robes, stand beside their King. When Jesus was preparing himself in the desert for the work of life, angels came to encourage him. Now, on the mountain, preparing himself for the work of death, Moses and Elijah draw near: Moses, the lawgiver whose grave no man knew; Elijah, the prophet who sidestepped death in a fiery chariot.

And then, the voice thunders. God inhabits a cloud. And from the belly of the cloud, the Father speaks: "This is my Son, whom I love; with him I am well pleased. Listen to him!"

For Peter, James, and John, the scene is bizarre: dazzling white clouds, a voice from the sky, living images from the past. But for Jesus, it is a view of home. A view into yesterday. A glimpse into tomorrow. And tomorrow's dream becomes today's courage.

JESUS HEALS A MAN AT THE POOL OF BETHESDA

Later Jesus went to Jerusalem for a special Jewish feast. In Jerusalem there is a pool with five covered porches, which is called [Bethesda].... Many sick people were lying on the porches beside the pool. Some were blind, some were crippled, and some were paralyzed. A man was lying there who had been sick for thirty-eight years. When Jesus saw the man and knew he had been sick for such a long time, Jesus asked him, "Do you want to be well?"

The sick man answered, "Sir, there is no one to help me get into the pool when the water starts moving. While I am coming to the water, someone else always gets in before me." Then Jesus said, "Stand up. Pick up your mat and walk."

JOHN 5:1-8

MAX LUCADO

Picture a battleground strewn with wounded bodies, and you see Bethesda. Imagine a nursing home overcrowded and understaffed, and you see the pool. Call to mind the orphans in Bangladesh or the abandoned in New Delhi, and you will see what people saw when they passed Bethesda. As they passed, what did they hear? An endless wave of groans. What did they witness? A faceless field of need. What did they do? Most walked past, ignoring the people.

But not Jesus. He is in Jerusalem for a feast. We don't know if he ever made it to the temple, but we do know he made it to Bethesda.

He is alone. He's not there to teach the disciples or to draw a crowd. The people need him—so he's there.

Can you picture it? Jesus walking among the suffering. What is he thinking? When an infected hand touches his ankle, what does he do? When a blind child stumbles in Jesus' path, does he reach down to catch the child? When a wrinkled hand extends for alms, how does Jesus respond?

Whether the watering hole is Bethesda or Bill's Bar...how does God feel when people hurt?

It's worth the telling of the story if all we do is watch him walk. It's worth it just to know he even came.

JESUS FEEDS
FIVE THOUSAND PEOPLE

*W*hen Jesus looked up and saw a large crowd coming toward him, he said to Philip,
"Where can we buy enough bread for all these people to eat?" (Jesus asked Philip this
question to test him, because Jesus already knew what he planned to do.)

Philip answered, "We would all have to work a
month to buy enough bread for each person to have only a little piece."

Another one of his followers, Andrew, Simon Peter's brother, said, "Here is a boy with five
loaves of barley bread and two little fish, but that is not enough for so many people."

Jesus said, "Tell the people to sit down." This was a very grassy place,
and about five thousand men sat down there. Then Jesus took the loaves of bread,
thanked God for them, and gave them to the people who were sitting there.
He did the same with the fish, giving as much as the people wanted.

JOHN 6:5–11

MAX LUCADO

*H*is lunch wasn't much. In fact, it wasn't anything compared to what was needed for more than five thousand people.

He probably wrestled with the silliness of it all. What was one lunch for so many? He probably asked himself if it was even worth the effort.

How far could one lunch go?

I think that's why he didn't give the lunch to the crowd. Instead he gave it to Jesus. Something told him that if he would plant the seed, God would grant the crop.

So he did.

The boy summoned his courage, got up off the grass, and walked into the circle of grownups. He must have been nervous. No one likes to appear silly.

Someone probably snickered.

If they didn't snicker, they shook their heads. "The little fellow doesn't know any better."

If they didn't shake their heads, they rolled their eyes.

But it wasn't the men's heads or eyes that the boy saw; he saw only Jesus.

JESUS WALKS ON WATER

That evening Jesus' followers went down to Lake Galilee.
It was dark now, and Jesus had not yet come to them. The followers got into a boat
and started across the lake to Capernaum. By now a strong wind was blowing, and the
waves on the lake were getting bigger. When they had rowed the boat about three or four
miles, they saw Jesus walking on the water, coming toward the boat. The followers were
afraid, but Jesus said to them, "It is I. Do not be afraid." Then they were glad to take him
into the boat. At once the boat came to land at the place where they wanted to go.

JOHN 6:16-21

MAX LUCADO

JESUS WALKS ON WATER

*S*uppose one of Jesus' disciples kept a journal. And suppose that disciple made an entry in the journal on the morning after the storm. Here is how it would read…I suppose:

In the midst of the sea, our boat bounced. The waves slapped it as easily as children would a ball. We were a twig in a whirlpool…a leaf in the wind. We were helpless.

"A ghost," someone screamed. A flash of lightning illuminated the sky. For a second I could see its face…his face. It was the Master!

He spoke: "Take courage! It is I. Don't be afraid." And, somehow, courage came.

"Lord, if it's you,…tell me to come to you on the water." The voice was Peter's. He wasn't being cocky. He was scared. He knew that the boat would soon go down. He knew that Jesus was standing up. And he knew where he wanted to be…where we all wanted to be.

"Come on," Jesus invited. So Peter climbed over the side and stepped onto the sea. Jesus radiated light at the end of the trail. Peter stepped toward the light like it

was his only hope. He was halfway there when we all heard the thunder. I saw his head turn. He looked up at the sky. And down he went. Boy did he yell!

A hand came through the water sheets and grabbed Peter. Lightning flashed again, and I could see the face of Jesus. Hurt covered his face. It was like he couldn't believe that we couldn't believe.

Before I knew it, he was in the boat with us. The winds hushed. It happened instantaneously. From chaos to calm.

This was no dream. I looked at the water. I looked at Peter. And then I looked at him.

And I did the only thing I could have done. I fell at his feet and worshiped. I had never seen Jesus as I saw him then. But what I witnessed last night, I know I'll never forget.

I saw God. It took a storm for me to see him. But I saw him. And I'll never be the same.

JESUS FORGIVES THE WOMAN TAKEN IN ADULTERY

The teachers of the law and the Pharisees brought a woman who had been caught in adultery. They forced her to stand before the people. They said to Jesus, "Teacher, this woman was caught having sexual relations with a man who is not her husband. The law of Moses commands that we stone to death every woman who does this. What do you say we should do?" They were asking this to trick Jesus so that they could have some charge against him.

But Jesus bent over and started writing on the ground with his finger. When they continued to ask Jesus their question, he raised up and said, "Anyone here who has never sinned can throw the first stone at her." Then Jesus bent over again and wrote on the ground.

Those who heard Jesus began to leave one by one, first the older men and then the others. Jesus was left there alone with the woman standing before him. Jesus raised up again and asked her, "Woman, where are they? Has no one judged you guilty?"

She answered, "No one, sir."

Then Jesus said, "I also don't judge you guilty. You may go now, but don't sin anymore."

JOHN 8:3-11

Twenty

he law of Moses commands that we stone to death every woman who does this. What do you say we should do?" (v. 5). Pretty cocky, this committee of high ethics. Pretty proud of themselves, these agents of righteousness. This will be a moment they long remember, the morning they foil and snag the mighty Nazarene.

What does Jesus do? Jesus writes in the sand. He stoops down and draws in the dirt. And as he writes, he speaks: "Anyone here who has never sinned can throw the first stone at her."

The young look to the old. The old look in their hearts. They are the first to drop their stones. And as they turn to leave, the young who were cocky with borrowed convictions do the same. The only sound is the thud of rocks and the shuffle of feet.

With the jury gone, the courtroom becomes the judge's chambers, and the woman awaits his verdict. "Woman, where are they? Has no one judged you guilty?" She answers, "No one, sir." Then Jesus says, "I also don't judge you guilty. You may go now, but don't sin anymore."

If you have ever wondered how God reacts when you fail, frame these words and hang them on the wall. Read them. Ponder them. Drink from them. Stand below them and let them wash over your soul.

And remember. Remember the message he left. Not in the sand, but on a cross. Not with his hand, but with his blood. His message has two words: Not guilty.

JESUS HEALS A CANAANITE WOMAN'S DAUGHTER

Jesus left that place and went to the area of Tyre and Sidon. A Canaanite woman from that area came to Jesus and cried out, "Lord, Son of David, have mercy on me! My daughter has a demon, and she is suffering very much."

But Jesus did not answer the woman. So his followers came to Jesus and begged him, "Tell the woman to go away. She is following us and shouting."

Jesus answered, "God sent me only to the lost sheep, the people of Israel."

Then the woman came to Jesus again and bowed before him and said, "Lord, help me!"

Jesus answered, "It is not right to take the children's bread and give it to the dogs."

The woman said, "Yes, Lord, but even the dogs eat the crumbs that fall from their masters' table."

Then Jesus answered, "Woman, you have great faith! I will do what you asked." And at that moment the woman's daughter was healed.

MATTHEW 15:21-28

MAX LUCADO

The disciples are annoyed. "Send her away," they demand. The spotlight is put on Jesus. And what follows is one of the most intriguing dialogues in the New Testament.

"I was sent only to the lost sheep of Israel," he says.

"Lord, help me!"

"It is not right to take the children's bread and toss it to their dogs," he answers.

"But even the dogs eat the crumbs that fall from their masters' table," she responds.

Is Jesus being rude? Is he calling this woman a dog? How do we explain this dialogue?

Could it be that Jesus' tongue is poking his cheek? Could Jesus be so delighted to have found one who is not bartering with a religious system or proud of a heritage that he can't resist a bit of satire? So he decides to engage in a humorous moment with a faithful woman.

In essence, here's what they said: "Now, you know that God only cares about Jews," he says smiling. And when she catches on, she volleys back, "But your bread is so precious, I'll be happy to eat the crumbs." In a spirit of exuberance, he bursts out, "Never have I seen such faith! Your daughter is healed."

This story does not portray a contemptuous God. It portrays a willing One who delights in a sincere seeker. Aren't you glad he does?

JESUS TEACHES FORGIVENESS

*T*hen Jesus said, "A man had two sons. The younger son said to his father,
'Give me my share of the property.' So the father divided the property between his two
sons. Then the younger son gathered up all that was his and traveled far away to another
country. There he wasted his money in foolish living. After he had spent everything, a time
came when there was no food anywhere in the country, and the son was poor and hungry.
So he got a job with one of the citizens there who sent the son into the fields to feed pigs.
The son was so hungry that he wanted to eat the pods the pigs were eating, but no one gave
him anything. When he realized what he was doing, he thought, 'All of my father's servants have plenty of food. But I am here, almost dying with hunger. I will leave and return
to my father and say to him, "Father, I have sinned against God and have done wrong to
you. I am no longer worthy to be called your son, but let me be like one of your servants."'
So the son left and went to his father.

"While the son was still a long way off, his father saw him and felt sorry for his son.
So the father ran to him and hugged and kissed him. The son said, 'Father, I have sinned
against God and have done wrong to you. I am no longer worthy to be called your son.'
But the father said to his servants, 'Hurry! Bring the best clothes and put them

MAX LUCADO

on him. Also, put a ring on his finger and sandals on his feet. And get our fat calf and kill it so we can have a feast and celebrate. My son was dead, but now he is alive again! He was lost, but now he is found!' So they began to celebrate.

"The older son was in the field, and as he came closer to the house, he heard the sound of music and dancing. So he called to one of the servants and asked what all this meant. The servant said, 'Your brother has come back, and your father killed the fat calf, because your brother came home safely.' The older son was angry and would not go in to the feast. So his father went out and begged him to come in. But the older son said to his father, 'I have served you like a slave for many years and have always obeyed your commands. But you never gave me even a young goat to have at a feast with my friends. But your other son, who wasted all your money on prostitutes, comes home, and you kill the fat calf for him!' The father said to him, 'Son, you are always with me, and all that I have is yours. We had to celebrate and be happy because your brother was dead, but now he is alive. He was lost, but now he is found.' "

LUKE 15:11-32

*T*he road home was longer than he remembered. When he last traveled it, he turned heads because of his style. If he turned heads this time it was because of his stink. His clothes were torn, his hair matted, and his feet black. But that didn't bother him, because for the first time in a calendar of heartaches, he had a clean conscience.

He was going home. Not demanding that he get what he deserved, but willing to take whatever he could get. "Give me" had been replaced with "help me," and his defiance had been replaced with repentance.

He had no money. He had no excuses. And he had no idea how much his father had missed him. He had no idea the number of times his father had paused between chores to look out the front gate for his son. The boy had no idea the number of times his father had awakened from restless sleep, gone into the son's room, and sat on the boy's bed.

As the boy came around the bend that led up to his house, he rehearsed his speech one more time. "Father, I have sinned against heaven and against you."

He approached the gate and placed his hand on the latch. He began to lift it, then he paused. His plan to go home suddenly seemed silly. "What's the use?" he heard himself asking himself.

Then he heard the footsteps. Someone was running. It's probably a servant coming to chase me away or my big brother wanting to know what I'm doing back home. He began to leave.

But the voice he heard was not the voice of a servant nor the voice of his brother; it was the voice of his father. "Son!" "Father?" Tears glistened on his cheeks as arms stretched from east to west inviting the son to come home.

"Father, I have sinned." The words were muffled as the boy buried his face in his father's shoulder. The two wept. Words were unnecessary. Repentance had been made, forgiveness had been given. The boy was home.

MAX LUCADO
FROM: *SIX HOURS ONE FRIDAY*

Twenty-Three

JESUS HEALS TEN LEPERS

*While Jesus was on his way to Jerusalem,
he was going through the area between Samaria and Galilee.
As he came into a small town, ten men who had a skin disease
met him there. They did not come close to Jesus but
called to him, "Jesus! Master! Have mercy on us!"*

*When Jesus saw the men, he said,
"Go and show yourselves to the priests."*

*As the ten men were going, they were healed.
When one of them saw that he was healed, he went back to Jesus,
praising God in a loud voice. Then he bowed down at Jesus' feet and
thanked him. (And this man was a Samaritan.) Jesus said,
"Weren't ten men healed? Where are the other nine?
Is this Samaritan the only one who came back to thank God?"
Then Jesus said to him, "Stand up and go on your way.
You were healed because you believed."*

LUKE 17:11-19

Those who know Christ most are the most grateful. I recently read a story of a woman who for years was married to a harsh husband. Each day he would leave her a list of chores to complete before he returned at the end of the day. "Clean the yard. Stack the firewood. Wash the windows...."

If she didn't complete the tasks, she would be greeted with his explosive anger. But even if she did complete the list, he was never satisfied; he would always find inadequacies in her work.

After several years, the husband passed away. Some time later she remarried, this time to a man who lavished her with tenderness and adoration.

One day, while going through a box of old papers, the wife discovered one of her first husband's lists. And as she read the sheet, a realization caused a tear of joy to splash on the paper.

"I'm still doing all these things, and no one has to tell me. I do it because I love him."

That is the unique characteristic of the new kingdom. Its subjects don't work in order to go to heaven: they work *because* they are going to heaven. Arrogance and fear are replaced with gratitude and joy.

MAX LUCADO
FROM: *THE APPLAUSE OF HEAVEN*

JESUS HEALS TEN LEPERS

JESUS ANSWERS A RICH MAN

As Jesus started to leave, a man ran to him
and fell on his knees before Jesus. The man asked,
"Good teacher, what must I do to have life forever?"

Jesus answered, "Why do you call me good?
Only God is good. You know the commands: 'You must not murder anyone.
You must not be guilty of adultery. You must not steal.
You must not tell lies about your neighbor.
You must not cheat. Honor your father and mother.' "

The man said, "Teacher, I have obeyed all these things since I was a boy."

Jesus, looking at the man, loved him and said,
"There is one more thing you need to do.
Go and sell everything you have, and give the money to the poor,
and you will have treasure in heaven.
Then come and follow me."

MARK 10:17-21

MAX LUCADO

Twenty-Four

All your life you've been rewarded according to your performance. You get grades according to your study. You get commendations according to your success. You get money in response to your work.

That's why the rich young ruler thought heaven was just a payment away. It only made sense. You work hard, you pay your dues, and "zap"—your account is credited as paid in full. Jesus said, "No way." What you want costs far more than what you can pay. You don't need a system, you need a Savior. You don't need a résumé, you need a Redeemer.

Mark it down. God does not save us because of what we've done. Only a puny god could be bought with tithes. Only an egotistical god would be impressed with our pain. Only a temperamental god could be satisfied by sacrifices. Only a heartless god would sell salvation to the highest bidders.

And only a great God does for his children what they can't do for themselves.

JESUS HEALS A BLIND MAN

As Jesus was walking along, he saw a man who had been born blind. His followers asked him, "Teacher, whose sin caused this man to be born blind—his own sin or his parents' sin?"

Jesus answered, "It is not this man's sin or his parents' sin that made him be blind. This man was born blind so that God's power could be shown in him...."

After Jesus said this, he spit on the ground and made some mud with it and put the mud on the man's eyes. Then he told the man, "Go and wash in the Pool of Siloam." (Siloam means Sent.) So the man went, washed, and came back seeing.

JOHN 9:1-7

John tells of a time the disciples applied a label. Jesus and his followers came upon a man who had been blind from birth. Here is the question the disciples asked Jesus: "Teacher, whose sin caused this man to be born blind—his own sin or his parents' sin?" (John 9:2).

Never mind that the man is a beggar in need of help. Never mind that the man has spent his life in a dark cave. Never mind that the man seated in front of them is in earshot of their voices. Let's talk about his sin. How could they be so harsh? So insensitive? So…blind.

The answer? (You may not like it.) It's easier to talk about a person than to help a person. It's easier to debate homosexuality than to be a friend to a gay person. It's easier to discuss divorce than to help the divorced. It's easier to argue abortion than to support an orphanage. It's easier to complain about the welfare system than to help the poor. It's easier to label than to love. It's especially easy to talk theology. Such discussions make us feel righteous. Self-righteous.

What if God did that with us? What if God judged us by our outward appearance? What if he judged us based on where we grew up? Or what we do for a living? Or the mistakes we made when we were young? He wouldn't do that, would he?

Jesus had another view of the man born blind. Rather than see him as an opportunity for discussion, he saw him as an opportunity for God. Why was he blind? "So God's power could be shown in him."

JESUS RAISES LAZARUS
FROM THE DEAD

Jesus said, "Move the stone away."

*Martha, the sister of the dead man, said,
"But, Lord, it has been four days since he died. There will be a bad smell."*

Then Jesus said to her, "Didn't I tell you that if you believed you would see the glory of God?"

*So they moved the stone away from the entrance. Then Jesus looked up and said,
"Father, I thank you that you heard me. I know that you always hear me, but I said these
things because of the people here around me. I want them to believe that you sent me."
After Jesus said this, he cried out in a loud voice, "Lazarus, come out!" The dead man
came out, his hands and feet wrapped with pieces of cloth, and a cloth around his face.*

Jesus said to them, "Take the cloth off of him and let him go."

. . .

*A large crowd of Jews heard that Jesus was in Bethany.
So they went there to see not only Jesus but Lazarus, whom Jesus raised from
the dead. So the leading priests made plans to kill Lazarus, too. Because of
Lazarus many of the Jews were leaving them and believing in Jesus.*

JOHN 11:39-44; 12:9-11

MAX LUCADO

Wow! Because of Lazarus many Jews were "believing in Jesus." Lazarus has been given a trumpet. He has a testimony to give—and what a testimony he has!

"I was always a good fellow," he would say. "I paid my bills. I loved my sisters. I even enjoyed being around Jesus. But I wasn't one of the followers. I didn't get as close as Peter and James and those guys. I kept my distance. Nothing personal. I just didn't want to get carried away.

"But then I got sick. And then I died. I mean, I died dead. Nothing left. Stone-cold. No life. No breath. Nothing. I died to everything. I saw life from the tomb. And then Jesus called me from the grave. When he spoke, my heart beat and my soul stirred, and I was alive again. And I want you to know he can do the same for you."

If God has called you to be a Lazarus, then testify. Remind the rest of us that we, too, have a story to tell. We, too, have neighbors who are lost. We, too, have died and been resurrected.

MARY WASHES JESUS' FEET
WITH HER HAIR

*Six days before the Passover Feast, Jesus went to Bethany,
where Lazarus lived. (Lazarus is the man Jesus raised from the dead.)
There they had a dinner for Jesus. Martha served the food, and Lazarus was
one of the people eating with Jesus. Mary brought in a pint of very expensive
perfume made from pure nard. She poured the perfume on Jesus' feet, and then
she wiped his feet with her hair. And the sweet smell from the perfume
filled the whole house.*

JOHN 12:1-3

MAX LUCADO

Twenty-Seven

*I*s Mary in the kitchen? No, she is playing her flute for Jesus. She is worshiping, for that is what she loves to do. But this time Martha doesn't object. She has learned that there is a place for praise and worship, and that is what Mary is doing. And what is Mary's part in the dinner? She brings a pint of very expensive perfume and pours it on Jesus' feet, then wipes his feet with her hair. The smell of the perfume fills the house, just like the sound of praise can fill a church.

An earlier Martha would have objected. Such an act was too lavish, too extravagant, too generous. But this mature Martha has learned that just as there is a place in the kingdom of God for sacrificial service, there is also a place for extravagant praise.

Marys are gifted with praise. They don't just sing; they worship. They don't simply attend church; they go to offer praise. They don't just talk about Christ; they radiate Christ. When I find a Mary, I'm quick to ask, "How do I get on your prayer list?"

We need them because we tend to forget how much God loves worship. Marys don't forget. They know that God wants to be known as a father. They know that a father likes nothing more than to have his children sit at his feet and spend time with him. Marys are good at that.

THE TRIUMPHAL ENTRY

THE TRIUMPHAL ENTRY

As Jesus and his followers were coming closer to Jerusalem, they stopped at Bethphage at the hill called the Mount of Olives. From there Jesus sent two of his followers and said to them, "Go to the town you can see there. When you enter it, you will quickly find a donkey tied there with its colt. Untie them and bring them to me. If anyone asks you why you are taking the donkeys, say that the Master needs them, and he will send them at once."

MATTHEW 21:1-3

hen we all get home I know
what I want to do. There's someone I want to get to know. You go ahead
and swap stories with Mary or talk doc-
trine with Paul. I'll catch up with you soon.
But first, I want to meet the guy with the
donkey.

I don't know his name or what he looks
like. I only know one thing: what he gave.
He gave a donkey to Jesus on the Sunday
he entered Jerusalem.

"Go to the town you can see there. When
you enter it, you will quickly find a donkey
tied there with its colt. Untie them and
bring them to me. If anyone asks you why
you are taking the donkeys, say that the
Master needs them, and he will send them
at once."

When we all get to heaven I want to visit
this fellow. I have several questions for him.

How did you know? How did you know
it was Jesus who needed a donkey? Did
you have a vision? Did you get a telegram?
Did an angel appear in your bowl of lentils?

Was it hard to give? Was it difficult to
give something to Jesus for him to use?
I want to ask that question because
sometimes it's hard for me. Sometimes
I like to keep my animals to myself.
Sometimes when God wants something
I act like I don't know he needs it.

How did it feel? How did it feel to look
out and see Jesus on the back of the donkey
that lived in your barn? Were you proud?
Were you surprised? Were you annoyed?

Did you know? Did you have any idea
that your generosity would be used for
such a noble purpose? Did it ever occur
to you that God was going to ride your
donkey? Were you aware that all four

Gospel writers would tell your story? Did it ever cross your mind that a couple of millenniums later, a curious preacher in South Texas would be pondering your plight late at night?

And as I ponder yours, I ponder mine. Sometimes I get the impression that God wants me to give him something and sometimes I don't give it because I don't know for sure, and then I feel bad because I've missed my chance. And other times, too few times, I hear him and I obey him and feel honored that a gift of mine would be used to carry Jesus into another place. And still other times I wonder if my little deeds today will make a difference in the long haul.

Maybe you have those questions, too. All of us have a donkey. You and I each have something in our lives, which, if given back to God, could, like the donkey, move Jesus and his story further down the road. Maybe you can sing or hug or program a computer or speak Swahili or write a check.

Whichever, that's your donkey.

Whichever, your donkey belongs to him.

It could be that God wants to mount your donkey and enter the walls of another city, another nation, another heart. Do you let him? Do you give it? Or do you hesitate?

That guy who gave Jesus the donkey is just one in a long line of folks who gave little things to a big God. Scripture has quite a gallery of donkey-givers. In fact, heaven may have a shrine to honor God's uncommon use of the common.

THE LESSON OF THE FIG TREE

*Early the next morning, as Jesus was going back to
the city, he became hungry. Seeing a fig tree beside the road,
Jesus went to it, but there were no figs on the tree, only leaves.
So Jesus said to the tree, "You will never again have fruit."
The tree immediately dried up.*

*When his followers saw this, they were amazed.
They asked, "How did the fig tree dry up so quickly?"*

*Jesus answered, "I tell you the truth, if you have faith
and do not doubt, you will be able to do what I did to this tree and even more.
You will be able to say to this mountain, 'Go, fall into the sea.'
And if you have faith, it will happen. If you believe, you will
get anything you ask for in prayer."*

MATTHEW 21:18-22

MAX LUCADO

Twenty-Nine

*J*esus, hungry and on his way to Jerusalem, stops to see if a fig tree has figs. It doesn't. It has the appearance of nutrition but offers nothing. It's all promise and no performance. The symbolism is too precise for Jesus to ignore.

He does to the tree on Monday morning what he will do to the temple on Monday afternoon: He curses it. Note, he's not angry at the tree. He's angry at what the tree represents. Jesus is disgusted by lukewarm, placid, vain believers who have pomp but no purpose. They have no fruit.

What's the point? God can't stomach lukewarm faith. He is angered by a religion that puts on a show but ignores the service—and that is precisely the religion he was facing during his last week. And the religion he had faced his entire ministry.

The message of the fig tree is not for all of us to have the same fruit. The message is for us to have some fruit. Not easy. Jesus knows that. "If you have faith and do not doubt, you will be able to do what I did to this tree and even more."

Faith in whom? Religion? Hardly. Religion is the hoax Jesus is out to disclose.

No, the faith is not in religion, the faith is in God. A hardy, daring faith which believes God will do what is right, every time. And that God will do what it takes—whatever it takes—to bring his children home.

He is the shepherd in search of his lamb. His legs are scratched, his feet are sore and his eyes are burning. He scales the cliffs and traverses the fields. He explores the caves. He cups his hands to his mouth and calls into the canyon.

And the name he calls is yours.

JESUS CLEARS THE TEMPLE

Thirty

JESUS CLEARS THE TEMPLE

Jesus went into the Temple and threw out all the people who were buying and selling there. He turned over the tables of those who were exchanging different kinds of money, and he upset the benches of those who were selling doves. Jesus said to all the people there, "It is written in the Scriptures, 'My Temple will be called a house for prayer.' But you are changing it into a 'hideout for robbers.'"

MATTHEW 21:12, 13

*I*t's a sad but true fact of the faith: religion is used for profit and prestige. When it is there are two results: people are exploited and God is infuriated.

There's no better example of this than what happened at the temple. After he had entered the city on the back of a donkey, Jesus "went into the Temple. After he had looked at everything, since it was already late, he went out to Bethany with the twelve apostles" (Mark 11:11).

The next morning when he returned, "Jesus went into the Temple and threw out all the people who were buying and selling there. He turned over the tables of those who were exchanging different kinds of money, and he upset the benches of those who were selling doves. Jesus said to the people there, 'It is written in the Scriptures, "My temple will be called a house for prayer." But you are changing it into a "hideout for robbers." ' "

It's not difficult to see what angered Jesus. Pilgrims journeyed days to see God, to witness the holy, to worship His Majesty. But before they were taken into the presence of God, they were taken to the cleaners.

Want to anger God? Get in the way of people who want to see him. Want to feel his fury? Exploit people in the name of God.

Mark it down. Religious hucksters poke the fire of divine wrath.

God will never hold guiltless those who exploit the privilege of worship.

MAX LUCADO
FROM: *AND THE ANGELS WERE SILENT*

JESUS WASHES HIS DISCIPLES' FEET

Jesus knew that the Father had given him power over everything
and that he had come from God and was going back to God.
So during the meal Jesus stood up and took off his outer clothing.
Taking a towel, he wrapped it around his waist. Then he poured
water into a bowl and began to wash the followers' feet,
drying them with the towel that was wrapped around him.

JOHN 13:3-5

JESUS WASHES HIS DISCIPLES' FEET

Thirty-One

I don't understand how God can be so kind to us, but he is. He kneels before us, takes our feet in his hands, and washes them. Please understand that in washing the disciples' feet, Jesus is washing ours. That's us being cleansed, not from our dirt, but from our sins.

And the cleansing is not just a gesture; it is a necessity. Listen to what Jesus said: "If I don't wash your feet, you are not one of my people" (John 13:8). Why not? Because we cannot. We cannot remove our own sin.

Don't miss the meaning here. To place our feet in the basin of Jesus is to place the filthiest parts of our lives into his hands. In the ancient East, people's feet were caked with mud and dirt. The servant of the feast saw to it that the feet were cleaned. Jesus is assuming the role of the servant. He will wash the grimiest part of your life.

If you let him. The water of the Servant comes only when we confess that we are dirty. Only when we confess that we are caked with filth, that we have walked forbidden trails and followed the wrong paths. We will never be cleansed until we confess we are dirty. And we will never be able to wash the feet of those who have hurt us until we allow Jesus, the one we have hurt, to wash ours.

THE LAST SUPPER

On the first day of the Feast of Unleavened Bread, the followers came to Jesus. They said, "Where do you want us to prepare for you to eat the Passover meal?"

Jesus answered, "Go into the city to a certain man and tell him, 'The Teacher says: The chosen time is near. I will have the Passover with my followers at your house.' " The followers did what Jesus told them to do, and they prepared the Passover meal.

In the evening Jesus was sitting at the table with his twelve followers....

While they were eating, Jesus took some bread and thanked God for it and broke it. Then he gave it to his followers and said, "Take this bread and eat it; this is my body."

Then Jesus took a cup and thanked God for it and gave it to the followers. He said, "Every one of you drink this. This is my blood which is the new agreement that God makes with his people. This blood is poured out for many to forgive their sins. I tell you this: I will not drink of this fruit of the vine again until that day when I drink it new with you in my Father's kingdom."

After singing a hymn, they went out to the Mount of Olives.

Matthew 26:17-20, 26-30

MAX LUCADO

When you read Matthew's account of the Last Supper, one incredible truth surfaces. Jesus is the person behind it all. It was Jesus who selected the place, designated the time, and set the meal in order. "The chosen time is near. I will have the Passover with my followers at your house."

And at the Supper, Jesus is not a guest, but the host: "and [Jesus] gave to the disciples." The subject of the verbs is the message of the event: "he took…he blessed…he broke…he gave…".

And, at the Supper, Jesus is not the served, but the servant. It is Jesus who, during the Supper, put on the garb of a servant and washed the disciples' feet.

Jesus is the most active one at the table. Jesus is not portrayed as the one who reclines and receives, but as the one who stands and gives. He still does. The Lord's Supper is a gift to you. The Lord's Supper is a sacrament, not a sacrifice.

Often, we think of the Supper as a performance, a time when we are on stage and God is the audience. A ceremony in which we do the work and he does the watching. That's not how it was intended. If it was, Jesus would have taken his seat at the table and relaxed.

That's not what he did. He, instead, fulfilled his role as a rabbi by guiding his disciples through the Passover. He fulfilled his role as a servant by washing their feet. And he fulfilled his role as a Savior by granting them forgiveness of sins.

He was in charge. He was on center stage. He was the person behind and in the moment.

And he still is.

JESUS REVEALS HIS AUTHORITY

Jesus said, "Don't let your hearts be troubled. Trust in God, and trust in me. There are many rooms in my Father's house; I would not tell you this if it were not true. I am going there to prepare a place for you. After I go and prepare a place for you, I will come back and take you to be with me so that you may be where I am.

You know the way to the place where I am going."

Thomas said to Jesus, "Lord, we don't know where you are going.
So how can we know the way?"

Jesus answered, "I am the way, and the truth, and the life. The only way to the Father is through me. If you really knew me, you would know my Father, too.
But now you do know him, and you have seen him."

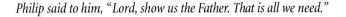

Philip said to him, "Lord, show us the Father. That is all we need."

Jesus answered, "I have been with you a long time now. Do you still not know me, Philip? Whoever has seen me has seen the Father. So why do you say, 'Show us the Father'? Don't you believe that I am in the Father and the Father is in me? The words I say to you don't come from me, but the Father lives in me and does his own work. Believe me when I say that I am in the Father and the Father is in me. Or believe because of the miracles I have done. I tell you the truth, whoever believes in me will do the same things that I do. Those who believe will do even greater things than these, because I am going to the Father. And if you ask for anything in my name, I will do it for you so that the Father's glory will be shown through the Son."

JOHN 14:1-13

Should a man see only popularity, he becomes a mirror, reflecting whatever needs to be reflected to gain acceptance. Though in vogue, he is vague. Though in style, he is stodgy. Personal convictions change with the seasons. Individual beliefs come in all colors, each for a different night of the week. He's a puppet on a thousand strings. He's a singer of a hundred songs, with no song of his own. His appearance changes to fit the setting so often that he forgets who he set out to be. He is everyone and no one.

Should a man see only power, he becomes a wolf—prowling, hunting, and stalking the elusive game. Recognition is his prey, and people are his prizes. His quest is endless. There is always another world to conquer or another person to control. As a result, he who sees only power is degraded to an animal, an insatiable scavenger, controlled not by a will from within but by lurings from without.

Should a man see only pleasure, he becomes a carnival thrill-seeker, alive only in bright lights, wild rides, and titillating entertainment. With lustful fever he races from ride to ride, satisfying his insatiable

MAX LUCADO

Thirty-Three

passion for sensations only long enough to look for another. Ferris wheels of romance. Haunted houses of eroticism. Hammer rides of danger and excitement. Long after the crowd is gone he can still be found on the carnival grounds rummaging through empty boxes of popcorn and sticky cones that held the cotton candy. He is driven by passion, willing to sell his soul if need be for one more rush, one more race of the pulse, one more sideshow that will take him away from the real world of promises broken and commitments to keep.

Seekers of popularity, power, and pleasure. The end result is the same: painful unfulfillment.

Only in seeing his Maker does a man truly become man. For in seeing his Creator man catches a glimpse of what he was intended to be. He who would see his God would then see the reason for death and the purpose of time. Destiny? Tomorrow? Truth? All are questions within the reach of the man who knows his source.

It is in seeing Jesus that man sees his Source.

JESUS PROCLAIMS HIS VICTORY OVER THE WORLD

"I have told you these things, using stories that hide the meaning. But the time will come when I will not use stories like that to tell you things; I will speak to you in plain words about the Father. In that day you will ask the Father for things in my name. I mean, I will not need to ask the Father for you. The Father himself loves you. He loves you because you loved me and believed that I came from God. I came from the Father into the world. Now I am leaving the world and going back to the Father."

Then the followers of Jesus said, "You are speaking clearly to us now and are not using stories that are hard to understand. We can see now that you know all things. You can answer a person's question even before it is asked. This makes us believe you came from God."

Jesus answered, "So now you believe? Listen to me; a time is coming when you will be scattered, each to his own home. That time is now here. You will leave me alone, but I am never really alone, because the Father is with me.

"I told you these things so that you can have peace in me. In this world you will have trouble, but be brave! I have defeated the world."

JOHN 16:25-33

MAX LUCADO

God will whisper. He will shout. He will touch and tug. He will take away our burdens; he'll even take away our blessings. If there are a thousand steps between us and him, he will take all but one. But he will leave the final one for us. The choice is ours.

Please understand. His goal is not to make you happy. His goal is to make you his. His goal is not to get you what you want; it is to get you what you need. And if that means a jolt or two to get your attention, then be jolted. Earthly discomfort is a glad swap for heavenly peace. Jesus said, "In this world you will have trouble, but be brave! I have defeated the world" (John 16:33).

How could he speak with such authority? What gave him the right to take command? Simple. He knows what we don't, and he can see what we can't.

What does God know? He knows how to navigate history.

God wants to get you home safely.

JESUS PRAYS IN
THE GARDEN OF GETHSEMANE

*Jesus went with his followers to a place called Gethsemane. He said to them,
"Sit here while I go over there and pray." He took Peter and the two sons of Zebedee
with him, and he began to be very sad and troubled. He said to them, "My heart
is full of sorrow, to the point of death. Stay here and watch with me."*

*After walking a little farther away from them, Jesus fell to the ground and prayed,
"My Father, if it is possible, do not give me this cup of suffering. But do what you want,
not what I want." Then Jesus went back to his followers and found them asleep.
He said to Peter, "You men could not stay awake with me for one hour?
Stay awake and pray for strength against temptation. The spirit wants
to do what is right, but the body is weak."*

MAX LUCADO

Then Jesus went away a second time and prayed, "My Father, if it is not possible for this painful thing to be taken from me, and if I must do it, I pray that what you want will be done."

Then he went back to his followers, and again he found them asleep, because their eyes were heavy. So Jesus left them and went away and prayed a third time, saying the same thing.

Then Jesus went back to his followers and said, "Are you still sleeping and resting? The time has come for the Son of Man to be handed over to sinful people. Get up, we must go. Look, here comes the man who has turned against me."

MATTHEW 26:36-46

My father taught me the lesson early: Don't create havoc in the garden. You can play ball in the yard. You can have races in the alley. You can build a fort in the tree. But the garden? Leave it alone.

I hate to think I have anything in common with the devil, but I guess I do. Satan learned the same lesson: Don't mess around with a garden—especially a garden that belongs to the Father.

The Bible is the story of two gardens. Eden and Gethsemane. In the first, Adam took a fall. In the second, Jesus took a stand. In the first, God sought Adam. In the second, Jesus sought God. In Eden, Adam hid from God. In Gethsemane, Jesus emerged from the dark. In Eden, Satan led Adam to a tree that led to his death. From Gethsemane, Jesus went to a tree that led to our life.

Satan was never invited to the Garden of Eden. He did not belong there. If he has invaded a garden of your life, then invite Jesus to reclaim it. Open the gate to God. He will enter and do what he did at Gethsemane. He will pray, and he will protect, and he will reclaim.

MAX LUCADO
FROM: *A GENTLE THUNDER*

Thirty-Six

JESUS IS ARRESTED

*K*nowing *everything that would happen to him, Jesus went*
out and asked, "Who is it you are looking for?"

They answered, "Jesus from Nazareth."

"I am he," Jesus said. (Judas, the one who turned against Jesus,
was standing there with them.) When Jesus said, "I am he," they moved back
and fell to the ground.

Jesus asked them again, "Who is it you are looking for?"

They said, "Jesus of Nazareth."

"I told you that I am he," Jesus said.
"So if you are looking for me, let the others go."

JOHN 18:4-8

emarkable. They stand only a few feet from his face and don't recognize him. Not even Judas realizes who stands before them. What a truth. Seeing Jesus is more than a matter of the eyes; it is a matter of the heart. The enemy is next to Jesus and doesn't realize it.

He reveals himself. "I am he." His voice flicks the first domino, and down they tumble. Were the moment not so solemn it would be comic. These are the best soldiers with Satan's finest plan; yet one word from Jesus, and they fall down! Don't miss the symbolism here: When Jesus speaks, Satan falls. Doesn't matter who the evil one has recruited. The best of Satan melts as wax before the presence of Christ.

Jesus has to ask them again whom they seek. "Who are you after?" When they answer that they are looking for Jesus of Nazareth, he instructs them, "So if you are looking for me, let the others go."

What is this?

Jesus commanding them! A Jew instructing a Roman? We turn to the commander, expecting a reply. But not only are they silent, they are obedient. The apostles are set free.

MAX LUCADO
FROM: A GENTLE THUNDER

PILATE QUESTIONS JESUS

Jesus stood before Pilate the governor, and Pilate asked him,
"Are you the king of the Jews?"

Jesus answered, "Those are your words."

When the leading priests and the older leaders accused Jesus, he said nothing.

So Pilate said to Jesus, "Don't you hear them accusing you of all these things?"

But Jesus said nothing in answer to Pilate, and Pilate was very surprised at this.

Every year at the time of Passover the governor would free one
prisoner whom the people chose. At that time there was a man in prison,
named Barabbas, who was known to be very bad. When the people gathered
at Pilate's house, Pilate said, "Whom do you want me to set free: Barabbas
or Jesus who is called the Christ?" Pilate knew that the people turned
Jesus in to him because they were jealous.

While Pilate was sitting there on the judge's seat, his wife sent this message to him:
"Don't do anything to that man, because he is innocent.
Today I had a dream about him, and it troubled me very much."

*But the leading priests and older leaders convinced the crowd to ask
for Barabbas to be freed and for Jesus to be killed.*

Pilate said, "I have Barabbas and Jesus. Which do you want me to set free for you?"

The people answered, "Barabbas."

Pilate asked, "So what should I do with Jesus, the one called the Christ?"

They all answered, "Crucify him!"

Pilate asked, "Why? What wrong has he done?"

But they shouted louder, "Crucify him!"

*When Pilate saw that he could do nothing about this and that a riot was starting, he took
some water and washed his hands in front of the crowd. Then he said, "I am not guilty of
this man's death. You are the ones who are causing it!"*

All the people answered, "We and our children will be responsible for his death."

*Then he set Barabbas free. But Jesus was beaten with whips and
handed over to the soldiers to be crucified.*

Matthew 27:11-26

MAX LUCADO

erhaps you, like Pilate, are curious about this one called Jesus. Pilate's question is yours. "What will I do with this man, Jesus?"

You have two choices. You can reject him. That is an option. You can, as have many, decide that the idea of God becoming a carpenter is too bizarre—and walk away. Or you can accept him. You can journey with him. You can listen for his voice amidst the hundreds of voices and follow him.

Pilate could have. He heard many voices that day—he could have heard Christ's. Had Pilate chosen to respond to this bruised Messiah, his story would have been different. Listen to his question: "Are you the king of the Jews?" Had we been there that day we would know the tone of voice Pilate used. Mockery? (You...the king?) Curiosity? (Who are you?) Sincerity? (Are you really who you say you are?) We wonder about his motive. So did Jesus.

"Is that your own question, or did others tell you about me?" Jesus wants to know why Pilate wants to know. What if Pilate had simply said, "I'm asking for myself. I want to know. I really want to know. Are you the king you claim to be?" If he had asked, Jesus would have told him. If he had asked, Jesus would have freed him. But Pilate didn't want to know. He just turned on his heel and retorted, "I am not Jewish." Pilate didn't ask so Jesus didn't tell.

Pilate vacillates. He is a puppy hearing two voices. He steps toward one, then stops, and steps toward the other. Four times he tries to free Jesus, and four times he is swayed otherwise. So many voices. The voice of compromise. The voice of expedience. The voice of politics. The voice of conscience. And the soft, firm voice of Christ. "The only power you have over me is the power given to you by God." Jesus' voice is distinct. Unique.

Pilate thought he could avoid making a choice. He washed his hands of Jesus. He climbed on the fence and sat down. But in not making a choice, Pilate made a choice. Rather than ask for God's grace, he asked for a bowl. Rather than invite Jesus to stay, he sent him away. Rather than hear Christ's voice, he heard the voice of the people.

Legend has it that Pilate's wife became a believer. And legend has it that Pilate's eternal home is a mountain lake where he daily surfaces, still plunging his hands into the water seeking forgiveness. Forever trying to wash away his guilt…not for the evil he did, but for the kindness he didn't do.

MAX LUCADO
FROM: *AND THE ANGELS WERE SILENT*

THE REPENTANT THIEF

There were also two criminals led out with Jesus to be put to death. When they came to a place called the Skull, the soldiers crucified Jesus and the criminals—one on his right and the other on his left. Jesus said, "Father, forgive them, because they don't know what they are doing."

The soldiers threw lots to decide who would get his clothes. The people stood there watching. And the leaders made fun of Jesus, saying, "He saved others. Let him save himself if he is God's chosen One, the Christ."

The soldiers also made fun of him, coming to Jesus and offering him some vinegar. They said, "If you are the king of the Jews, save yourself!" At the top of the cross these words were written:
THIS IS THE KING OF THE JEWS.

One of the criminals on a cross began to shout insults at Jesus:
"Aren't you the Christ? Then save yourself and us."

But the other criminal stopped him and said,
"You should fear God! You are getting the same punishment he is.
We are punished justly, getting what we deserve for what we did.
But this man has done nothing wrong." Then he said, "Jesus, remember me
when you come into your kingdom."

Jesus said to him, "I tell you the truth, today you will be with me in paradise."

LUKE 23:32-43

MAX LUCADO

The first criminal reads the sign that announces Jesus as the king of the Jews. He hears Jesus pray for those who kill him. Something about the presence of the carpenter convinces him he's in the presence of a king.

The other crook has a different opinion. "Aren't you the Christ? Then save yourself and us." You'd think a man near death would use his energy for something other than slander. Not this one. The shadow over his heart is so thick, even in pain he mocks.

Suddenly someone tells him, "You should fear God!" It's the voice of the first criminal. "We are getting what we deserve for what we did. But this man has done nothing wrong."

Finally someone is defending Jesus. Peter fled. The disciples hid. The Jews accused. Pilate washed his hands. Many could have spoken on behalf of Jesus, but none did. Until now. Kind words from the lips of a thief. He makes his request. "Jesus, remember me when you come into your kingdom."

The Savior turns his heavy head toward the prodigal child and promises, "I tell you the truth, today you will be with me in paradise."

To those at the foot of the cross, the dialogue was curious. They couldn't imagine it. How could the thief come to paradise? How could a soul speckled by sin go to heaven? How could a sinner be saved?

It is eternity's most bizarre exchange. Paul explained it like this: "Christ took away the curse the law put on us. He changed places with us and put himself under that curse" (Gal. 3:13).

JESUS' CRUCIFIXION

At noon the whole country became dark, and the darkness lasted for three hours. At three o'clock Jesus cried in a loud voice, "Eloi, Eloi, lama sabachthani." This means, "My God, my God, why have you rejected me?"

When some of the people standing there heard this, they said, "Listen! He is calling Elijah."

Someone there ran and got a sponge, filled it with vinegar, tied it to a stick, and gave it to Jesus to drink. He said, "We want to see if Elijah will come to take him down from the cross."

Then Jesus cried in a loud voice and died.

The curtain in the Temple was torn into two pieces, from the top to the bottom. When the army officer who was standing in front of the cross saw what happened when Jesus died, he said, "This man really was the Son of God!"

MARK 15:33-39

JESUS' CRUCIFIXION

They killed him. He left as he came—penniless. He was buried in a borrowed grave, his funeral financed by compassionate friends. Though he once had everything, he died with nothing.

He should have been miserable. He should have been bitter. He had every right to be a pot of boiling anger. But he wasn't. He was joyful.

Sourpusses don't attract a following. People followed him wherever he went. Children avoid soreheads. Children scampered after this man. Crowds don't gather to listen to the woeful. Crowds clamored to hear him.

Why? He was joyful. He was joyful when he was poor. He was joyful when he was abandoned. He was joyful when he was betrayed. He was even joyful as he hung on a tool of torture, his hands pierced with six-inch Roman spikes. Jesus embodied a stubborn joy. A joy that refused to bend in the wind of hard times. A joy that held its ground against pain. A joy whose roots extended deep into the bedrock of eternity.

What type of joy is this? What is this cheerfulness that dares to wink at adversity? What is this bird that sings while it is still dark? What is the source of this peace that defies pain?

I call it sacred delight. It is sacred because it is not of the earth. What is sacred is God's. And this joy is God's.

MAX LUCADO

FROM: *THE APPLAUSE OF HEAVEN*

Forty

THE RESURRECTION

*A*t that time there was a strong earthquake. An angel of the Lord came
down from heaven, went to the tomb, and rolled the stone away from the entrance.
Then he sat on the stone. He was shining as bright as lightning, and his clothes were
white as snow. The soldiers guarding the tomb shook with fear because of
the angel, and they became like dead men.

The angel said to the women, "Don't be afraid. I know that you are looking for Jesus,
who has been crucified. He is not here. He has risen from the dead as he said he would.
Come and see the place where his body was. And go quickly and tell his followers,
'Jesus has risen from the dead. He is going into Galilee ahead of you, and you
will see him there.'" Then the angel said, "Now I have told you."

The women left the tomb quickly. They were afraid, but they were also very happy.
They ran to tell Jesus' followers what had happened. Suddenly, Jesus met them and said,
"Greetings." The women came up to him, took hold of his feet, and worshiped him.
Then Jesus said to them, "Don't be afraid. Go and tell my followers
to go on to Galilee, and they will see me there."

MATTHEW 28:2-10

hy did the angel move the stone? For whom did he roll away the rock?

For Jesus? Did the stone have to be removed in order for Jesus to exit? Did God have to help? Was the death conqueror so weak that he couldn't push away a rock?

I don't think so.

Listen to what the angel says: "Come and see the place where his body was."

The stone was moved—not for Jesus—but for the women; not so Jesus could come out, but so the women could see in!

Mary looks at Mary and Mary is grinning the same grin she had when the bread and fish kept coming out of the basket.

Suddenly it's all right to dream again.

"Go quickly and tell his followers, 'Jesus has risen from the dead. He is going into Galilee ahead of you, and you will see him there.'"

Mary and Mary don't have to be told twice. The sun is up. The Son is out. But the Son isn't finished.

One surprise still awaits them.

"Suddenly, Jesus met them and said, 'Greetings.' The women came up to him, took hold of his feet, and worshiped him. Then Jesus said to them, 'Don't be afraid. Go and tell my followers to go on to Galilee, and they will see me there.'"

MAX LUCADO
FROM: *HE STILL MOVES STONES*

THE ROAD TO EMMAUS

That same day two of Jesus' followers were going to a town named Emmaus,
about seven miles from Jerusalem. They were talking about everything that had happened.
While they were talking and discussing, Jesus himself came near and began
walking with them, but they were kept from recognizing him. Then he said,
"What are these things you are talking about while you walk?"

The two followers stopped, looking very sad. The one named Cleopas answered,
"Are you the only visitor in Jerusalem who does not know
what just happened there?"

Jesus said to them, "What are you talking about?"

They said, "About Jesus of Nazareth. He was a prophet who said and
did many powerful things before God and all the people. Our leaders and the leading
priests handed him over to be sentenced to death, and they crucified him.
But we were hoping that he would free Israel...."

*Then Jesus said to them, "You are foolish and slow to believe
everything the prophets said. They said that the Christ must suffer these
things before he enters his glory." Then starting with what Moses and all the
prophets had said about him, Jesus began to explain everything that had
been written about himself in the Scriptures.*

*They came near the town of Emmaus, and Jesus acted as if he were going farther.
But they begged him, "Stay with us, because it is late; it is almost night."
So he went in to stay with them.*

*When Jesus was at the table with them,
he took some bread, gave thanks,
divided it, and gave it to them.
And then, they were allowed to recognize Jesus.*

LUKE 24:13-31

MAX LUCADO

Two disciples are walking down the dusty road to the village of Emmaus. Their talk concerns the crucified Jesus. "I can hardly believe it. He's gone." "What do we do now?"

Just then a stranger comes up from behind and says, "I'm sorry, but I couldn't help overhear you. Who are you discussing?" They stop and turn.

One of them asks, "Where have you been the last few days? Haven't you heard about Jesus of Nazareth? And he continues to tell what has happened.

This scene fascinates me—two sincere disciples telling how the last nail has been driven in Israel's coffin. God, in disguise, listens patiently, his wounded hands buried deeply in his robe.

He must have been touched at the faithfulness of this pair. Yet he also must have been a bit chagrined. He had just gone to hell and back to give heaven to earth, and these two were worried about the political situation of Israel.

"But we had hoped that he was the one who was going to redeem Israel."

Words painted gray with disappointment. What we wanted didn't come. What came, we didn't want. The result? Shattered hope. The foundation of their world trembles.

We are not much different than burdened travelers, are we?

Our problem is not so much that God doesn't give us what we hope for as it is that we don't know the right thing for which to hope. (You may want to read that sentence again.)

Hope is not a granted wish or a favor performed; no, it is far greater than that. It is a zany, unpredictable dependence on a God who loves to surprise us out of our socks and be there in the flesh to see our reaction. ✝

JESUS CALLS PAUL

*In Jerusalem Saul was still threatening the followers of the Lord by
saying he would kill them. So he went to the high priest and asked him
to write letters to the synagogues in the city of Damascus. Then if Saul found
any followers of Christ's Way, men or women, he would arrest
them and bring them back to Jerusalem.*

*So Saul headed toward Damascus. As he came near the city,
a bright light from heaven suddenly flashed around him.
Saul fell to the ground and heard a voice saying to him,
"Saul, Saul! Why are you persecuting me?"*

Saul said, "Who are you, Lord?"

*The voice answered, "I am Jesus, whom you are persecuting.
Get up now and go into the city.
Someone there will tell you what you must do."*

ACTS 9:1-6

MAX LUCADO

JESUS CALLS PAUL

*B*lue-blooded and wild-eyed, this young zealot was hell-bent on keeping the kingdom pure—and that meant keeping the Christians out. He marched through the countryside like a general demanding that backslidden Jews salute the flag of the motherland or kiss their family and hopes good-bye.

All this came to a halt, however, on the shoulder of a highway. Equipped with subpoenas, handcuffs, and a posse, Paul was on his way to do a little personal evangelism in Damascus. That's when someone slammed on the stadium lights, and he heard the voice.

When he found out whose voice it was, his jaw hit the ground, and his body followed. He braced himself for the worst.

Jesus could have finished him on the road. He could have left him for the buzzards.

He could have sent him to hell. But he didn't. He sent him to the lost.

Paul himself called it crazy. He described it with phrases like "stumbling block" and "foolishness," but chose in the end to call it "grace."

And he defended his unquenchable loyalty by saying, "The love of Christ leaves [me] no choice" (2 Cor. 5:14).

The message is gripping: Show a man his failures without Jesus, and the result will be found in the roadside gutter. Give a man religion without reminding him of his filth, and the result will be arrogance in a three-piece suit. But get the two in the same heart—get sin to meet Savior and Savior to meet sin—and the result just might be another Pharisee turned preacher who sets the world on fire.

MAX LUCADO
FROM: *THE APPLAUSE OF HEAVEN*

A VIEW OF HEAVEN

So we do not give up. Our physical body is becoming older and weaker, but our spirit inside us is made new every day. We have small troubles for a while now, but they are helping us gain an eternal glory that is much greater than the troubles. We set our eyes not on what we see but on what we cannot see. What we see will last only a short time, but what we cannot see will last forever.

2 CORINTHIANS 4:16-18

While in Colorado for a week's vacation, our family teamed up with several others and decided to ascend the summit of a fourteen-thousand-foot peak. We would climb it the easy way. Drive above the timberline and tackle the final mile by foot. You hearty hikers would have been bored, but for a family with three small girls, it was about all we could take.

The journey was as tiring as it was beautiful. I was reminded how the air was thin and my waist was not.

Our four-year-old Sara had it doubly difficult. A tumble in the first few minutes left her with a skinned knee and a timid step. She didn't want to walk. Actually, she *refused* to walk. She wanted to ride. First on my back, then in Mom's arms, then my back, then a friend's back, then my back, then Mom's...well, you get the picture.

In fact, you know how she felt. You, too, have tumbled, and you, too have asked for help. And you, too, have received it.

All of us need help sometimes. This journey gets steep. So steep that some of us give up. Some stop climbing. They haven't abandoned the trip, but they haven't continued it. They have simply stopped walking. Some will sit in the same place for years. They will not change. Prayers will not deepen. Devotion will not increase. Passion will not rise.

A few even grow cynical. Woe to the prophet who dares them to see the mountain. Woe to the explorer who reminds them of their call...pilgrims are not welcome here. And so the pilgrim moves on while the settler settles. Settles for sameness. Settles for safety. Settles for snowdrifts.

I hope you don't do that. But if you do, I hope you don't scorn the pilgrim who calls you back to the journey. It's worth it to keep moving.

As I tried, unsuccessfully, to convince Sara to walk, I tried describing what we were going to see. "It will be so pretty," I told her. "You'll see all the mountains and the sky and the trees." No luck—she wanted to be carried.

By the way, a grand scene awaits you as well. The Hebrew writer gives us a *National Geographic* piece on heaven. Listen to how he describes the mountaintop of Zion. He says when we reach the mountain we will have come to "the city of the living God.... To thousands of angels gathered together with joy.... To the meeting of God's first-born children whose names are written in heaven.... To God, the judge of all people,...and to the spirits of good people who have been made perfect.... To Jesus, the One who brought the new agreement

from God to his people.... To the sprinkled blood that has a better message than the blood of Abel" (Heb. 12:22-24).

What a mountain! Won't it be great to see the angels? To finally know what they look like and who they are? To hear them tell of the times they were at our side, even in our house?

Imagine the meeting of the firstborn. A gathering of all God's children. No jealousy. No competition. No division. No hurry. We will be perfect...sinless.

And imagine seeing God. Finally, to gaze in the face of your Father. To feel the Father's gaze upon you.

He will do what he promised he would do. *I will make all things new,* he promised. *I will restore what was taken. I will restore the smiles faded by hurt. I will replay the symphonies unheard by deaf ears and the sunsets unseen by blind eyes.*

The mute will sing. The poor will feast.

I will make all things new. New hope. New faith. And most of all new Love. The Love before which all other loves pale. The Love you have sought in a thousand ports in a thousand nights...this Love of mine, will be yours.

What a mountain! Jesus will be there. You've longed to see him. You finally will. Interesting what the writer says we will see. He doesn't mention the face of Jesus, though we will see it. He doesn't refer to the voice of Jesus, though it will shout. He mentions a part of Jesus that most of us wouldn't think of seeing. He says we will see Jesus' blood. The crimson of the cross. The life liquid that seeped from his forehead, dripped from his hands, and flowed from his side. The human blood of the divine Christ. Covering our sins. Proclaiming a message: *We have been bought. We cannot be sold. Ever.*

My, what a moment. What a mountain.

Believe me when I say it will be worth it. No cost is too high. Whatever it takes, do it. For heaven's sake, do it. It will be worth it. I promise. One view of the peak will justify the pain of the path.

By the way, our group finally made it up the mountain. We spent an hour or so at the top, taking pictures and enjoying the view. Later, on the way down, I heard little Sara exclaim proudly, "I did it!"

I chuckled. *No you didn't,* I thought. *Your mom and I did it. Friends and family got you up this mountain. You didn't do it.*

But I didn't say anything. I didn't say anything because I'm getting the same treatment. So are you. We may think we are climbing, but we are riding. Riding on the back of the Father who wants us to make it home. A Father who doesn't get angry when we get weary.

After all, he knows what it's like to climb a mountain. He climbed one for us.

MAX LUCADO

FROM: *WHEN GOD WHISPERS YOUR NAME*

YOUR GREATEST MOMENT

*Everyone who has ears should listen
to what the Spirit says to the churches.*

*I will give some of the hidden manna to everyone
who wins the victory. I will also give to each one who
wins the victory a white stone with a new name written on it.
No one knows this new name except
the one who receives it.*

REVELATION 2:17

I can't say I've given a lot of thought to my given name. Never figured it made much difference. I do recall a kid in elementary school wondering if I were German. I said no. "Then why do you have a German name?" I didn't even know Max was German. So I decided to find out.

"Why did you name me Max?" I asked Mom when I got home.

She looked up from the sink and replied, "You just looked like one."

Like I say, I haven't given much thought to my name. But there is one name that has caught my interest lately. A name only God knows. A name only God gives. A unique, one-of-a-kind, once-to-be-given name.

What am I talking about? Well, you may not have known it, but God has a new name for you. The name you've always heard won't be the one he uses. When God says he will make all things new, he means it. You will have a new home, a new body, a new life, and you guessed it, a new name.

Makes sense. Fathers are fond of giving their children special names. Princess. Tiger. Sweetheart. Bubba. Angel. I have a friend whose father calls her Willy. Her name is Priscilla. That became Silly-Willy. Today he calls her Willy. No one else does. Even if they did, no one else could say it the way her dad does.

Now maybe you didn't get a special name. Or maybe you have received special names. Names you never sought. Names of derision and hurt. Names like "loser" or "cheat," "cripple," "infected," or "divorced." If so, I'm sorry. You know how a name can hurt. But you can also imagine how a name can heal.

Especially when it comes from the lips of God. Isn't it incredible to think that God has saved a name just for you?

Imagine what that implies. Apparently your future is so promising it warrants a new title.

Your eternity is so special no common name will do. So God has one reserved just for you. There is more to your life than you ever thought. There is more to your story than what you have read. There is more to your song than what you have sung. The best is yet to be.

And so I urge you, don't give up. And so I plead, finish the journey. And so I exhort, be there. Be there when God whispers your name.

Acknowledgments

Max Lucado, *And the Angels Were Silent*,
Questar Publishers, Multnomah Books,
copyright 1992 by Max Lucado.

Max Lucado, *The Applause of Heaven*,
Word Inc., Dallas, Texas,
copyright 1990, 1995 by Max Lucado.

Max Lucado, *A Gentle Thunder*,
Word Inc., Dallas, Texas,
copyright 1995 by Max Lucado.

Max Lucado, *God Came Near*,
Questar Publishers, Multnomah Books,
copyright 1987.

Acknowledgments

Max Lucado, *He Still Moves Stones,*
Word Inc., Dallas, Texas,
copyright 1993 by Max Lucado.

Max Lucado, *In the Eye of the Storm,*
Word Inc., Dallas, Texas,
copyright 1991 by Max Lucado.

Max Lucado, *Six Hours One Friday,*
Questar Publishers, Multnomah Books,
copyright 1989 by Max Lucado.

Max Lucado, *When God Whispers Your Name,*
Word Inc, Dallas, Texas,
copyright 1994 by Max Lucado.